ISBN 978-0-265-58644-0
PIBN 10871225

THE LATTER-DAY SAINTS'

MILLENNIAL STAR.

[ESTABLISHED 1840.]

"If we resolve that to-morrow we shall live better, the resolution is in vain, for if we are too weak to begin now, our weakness by to-morrow will have so increased that a chain is made into a cable."

No. 50, Vol. LXXII. Thursday, December 15, 1910. Price One Penny.

THE TESTIMONY OF THE MONUMENTS TO THE TRUTH OF THE SCRIPTURES.

BY PROFESSOR GEORGE FREDERICK WRIGHT, D.D., LL.D., OBERLIN COLLEGE, U.S.A.

(Concluded from page 774.)

ACCURACY OF GEOGRAPHICAL DETAILS.

Many persons doubtless wonder why it is that the Bible so abounds in "uninteresting" lists of names both of persons and places which seem to have no relation to modern times or current events. Such, however, will cease to wonder when they come to see the relation which these lists sustain to our confidence in the trustworthiness of the records containing them. They are like the water-marks in paper, which bear indelible evidence of the time and place of manufacture. If, furthermore, one should contemplate personal explorations in Egypt, Canaan or Babylonia, he would find that for his purposes the most interesting and important portions of the Bible would be these very lists of the names of persons and places which seemed to encumber the historical books of the Old Testament.

One of the most striking peculiarities of the Bible is the "long look" toward the permanent wants of mankind which is everywhere manifested in its preparation; so that it circulates best in its entirety. No man knows enough to abridge the Bible without impairing its usefulness. The parts which the reviser would cut out as superfluous are sure, very soon, to be found to be "the more necessary." If we find that we have not any use for any portion of the Bible, the reason doubtless is that we have not lived long enough, or have not had sufficiently wide experience to test its merits in all particulars.

Gezer was an important place in Joshua's time, but it afterward became a heap of ruins, and its location was unknown until 1870, when M. Claremont-Ganneau discovered the site in Tel Jezer, and, on excavating it, found three inscriptions, which on interpretation read, "Boundary of Gezer."

Among the places conquered by Joshua, one of the most important and difficult to capture was Lachish (Josh. 10: 31). This has but recently been identified in Tel el-Hesy, about eighteen miles northeast of Gaza. Extensive excavations, first in 1890 by Dr. Flinders Petrie, and finally by Dr. Bliss, found a succession of ruins, one below the other, the lower foundations of which extended back to about 1700 B.C., some time before the period of the conquest, showing at that time a walled city of great strength. In the debris somewhat higher than this there was found a tablet with cuneiform inscriptions corresponding to the Tel el-Amarna tablets, which are known to have been sent to Egypt from this region about 1400 B.C. At a later period, in the time of Sennacherib, Lachish was assaulted and taken by the Assyrian army, and the account of the siege forms one of the most conspicuous scenes on the walls of Sennacherib's palace at Nineveh. These sculptures are now in the British Museum.

Among the places mentioned in the Tel el-Amarna correspondence from which letters were sent to Egypt about 1400 B.C., are Gebal, Beirut, Tyre, Accho (Acre), Hazor, Joppha, Ashkelon, Makkadah, Lachish, Gezer, Jerusalem; while mention is also made of Rabbah, Sarepta, Ashtaroth, Gaza, Gath, Bethshemesh, all of which are familiar names, showing that the Palestine of Joshua is the Palestine known to Egypt in the preceding century. Two hundred years before this (about 1600 B.C.) also, Thothmes III. conquered Palestine, and gives in an inscription the names of more than fifty towns which can be confidently identified with those in the Book of Joshua.

Finally, the forty-two stations named in Numbers 33 as camping places for the children of Israel on their way to Palestine, while they cannot all of them be identified, can be determined in sufficient numbers to show that it is not a fictitious list, nor a mere pilgrim's diary, since the scenes of greatest interest, like the region immediately about Mount Sinai, are specially adapted to the great transactions which are recorded as taking place. Besides, it is incredible that a writer of fiction should have encumbered his pages with such a barren catalogue of places. But as part of the great historical movement they are perfectly appropriate.

This conformity of newly discovered facts to the narrative of Sacred Scripture confirms our confidence in the main testimony; just as the consistency of a witness in a cross-examination upon minor and incidental points establishes confidence in his general testimony. The late Sir Walter Besant, in addition to his other literary and and philanthropic labors, was for many years secretary for the Palestine Exploration Fund. In reply to the inquiry whether the work of the survey under his direction sustained the historical character of the Old Testament, he says: "To my mind, absolute truth in local details, a thing which cannot possibly be invented, when it is spread over a history covering many centuries, is proof almost absolute as to the truth of the things related." Such proof we have for every part of the Bible.

THE FOURTEENTH OF GENESIS.

The fourteenth chapter of Genesis relates that "In the days of Amraphel, king of Shinar, Arioch, king of Ellasar, Chedorlaomer, king of Elam, and Tidal, king of Goiim (nations), they made war with Bera, king of Sodom, and with Bersha, king of Gomorrah, and Shinab, king of Admuh, and Shemeber, king of Zeboim, and the king of Bela (the same is Zoar)." The Babylonian kings were successful and the region about the Dead Sea was subject to them for twelve years, when a rebellion was instigated and in the following year Chedorlaomer and the kings that were with him appeared on the scene and, after capturing numerous surrounding cities joined battle with the rebellious allies in the vale of Siddim, which was full of slime pits. The victory of Chedorlaomer was complete, and after capturing Lot and his goods in Sodom he started homeward by way of Damascus, near which place Abraham overtook him, and by a successful stratagem scattered his forces by night and recovered Lot and his goods. This story, told with so many details that its refutation would be easy if it were not true to the facts and if there were contemporary records with which to compare it, has been a special butt for the ridicule of the Higher Critics of the Wellhausen school, Professor Nöldeke confidently declaring as late as 1869 that criticism had forever disproved its claim to be historical. But here again the inscriptions on the monuments of Babylonia have come to the rescue of the sacred historian, if indeed, he were in need of rescue. (For where general ignorance was so profound as it was respecting that period forty years ago, true modesty should have suggested caution in the expression of positive opinions in contradiction to such a detailed historical statement as this is.)

From the inscriptions already discovered and deciphered in the Valley of the Euphrates, it is now shown beyond reasonable doubt that the four kings mentioned in the Bible as joining in this expedition are not, as was freely said, "etymological inventions," but real historical persons. Amraphel is identified as the Hammurabi whose marvelous code of laws was so recently discovered by De Morgan at Susa. The "H" in the latter word simply expresses the rough breathing so well known in Hebrew. The "p" in the biblical name has taken the place of "b" by a well-recognized law of phonetic change. "Amrap" is equivalent to "Hamrab." The addition of "il" in the biblical name is probably the suffix of the divine name, like "el" in Israel.

Hammurabi is now known to have had his capital at Babylon at the time of Abraham. Until recently this chronology was disputed, so that the editors and contributors of the *New Schaff-Herzog Cyclopedia* dogmatically asserted that as Abraham lived nearly 300 years later than Hammurabi, the biblical story must be unhistorical. Hardly had these statements been printed, however, when Dr. King of the British Museum discovered indisputable evidence that two of the dynasties which formerly had been reckoned as consecutive were, in fact, contemporaneous, thus making it easy to bring Hammurabi's time down exactly to that of Abraham.

Chedorlaomer is pretty certainly identified as Kudur-Lagamar (servant of Lagamar, one of the principal Elamite gods). Kudur-Lagamar was king of Elam, and was either the father or the brother of Kudur-Mabug, whose son, Eri-Aku (Arioch), reigned over Larsa and Ur, and other cities of southern Babylonia. He speaks of Kudur-Mabug "as father of the land of the Amorites," *i.e.*, of Palestine and Syria.

Tidal, "king of nations," was supposed by Dr. Pinches to be referred to on a late tablet in connection with Chedorlaomer and Arioch under the name of Tudghula, who are said, together, to have "attacked and spoiled Babylon."

However much doubt there may be about the identification of some of these names, the main points are established, revealing a condition of things just such as is implied by the biblical narrative. Arioch styles himself king of Shumer and Accad, which embraced Babylon, where Amraphel (Hammurabi) was in his early years subject to him. This furnishes a reason for the association of Chedorlaomer and Amraphel in a campaign against the rebellious subjects in Palestine. Again, Kubur-Mabug, the father of Arioch, styles himself "Prince of the land of Amurru," *i.e.*, of Palestine and Syria. Moreover, for a long period before, kings from Babylonia had claimed possession of the whole eastern shore of the Mediterranean, including the Sinaitic Peninsula.

In light of these well-attested facts, one reads with astonishment the following words of Wellhausen, written no longer ago than 1889: "That four kings from the Persian Gulf should, 'in the time of Abraham,' have made an incursion into the Sinaitic Peninsula, that they should on this occasion have attacked five kinglets on the Dead Sea Littoral and have carried them off prisoners, and finally that Abraham should have set out in pursuit of the retreating victors, accompanied by 318 men servants, and have forced them to disgorge their prey—all these incidents are sheer impossibilities which gain nothing in credibility from the fact that they are placed in a world which had passed away."

And we can have little respect for the logic of a later scholar (George Adam Smith), who can write the following: "We must admit that while archæology has richly illustrated the possibility of the main outlines of the Book of Genesis from Abraham to Joseph, it has not one whit of proof to offer for the personal existence or the characters of the patriarchs themselves. This is the whole change archæology has wrought; it has given us a background and an atmosphere for the stories of Genesis; it is unable to recall or certify their heroes."

But the name Abraham does appear in tablets of the age of Hammurabi. (See Professor George Barton in Journal of Biblical Literature, Vol. 28, 1909, page 153.) It is true that this evidently is not the Abraham of the Bible, but that of a small farmer who had rented land of a well-to-do land owner. The preservation of his name is due to the fact that the most of the tablets preserved contain contracts relating to the business of the times. There is little reason to expect that we should find a definite reference to the Abraham who in early life migrated from his native land. But it is of a good deal of significance that his name appears to have been a common one in the time and place of his nativity.

In considering the arguments in the case, it is important to keep in mind that where so few facts are known, and general ignorance is so great, negative evidence is of small account, while every scrap of positive evidence has great weight. The burden of proof in such cases falls upon those who dispute the positive evidence. For example, in the article above referred to, Professor Barton argues that it is not "quite certain" that Arioch (Eri-Agu) was a real Babylonian king. But he admits that our ignorance is such that we must admit its "possibility." Dr. Barton further argues that "we have as yet no evidence from the inscriptions that Arad-Sin, even if he were called Iri-Agu, ever had anything to do with Hammurabi." But, he adds, "Of course, it is possible that he may have had, as their reigns must have overlapped, but that remains to be proved."

All such reasoning (and there is any amount of it in the critics of the prevalent school) reveals a lamentable lack in their logical training. When we have a reputable document containing positive historical statements which are shown by circumstantial evidence to be possible, that is all we need to accept them as true. When, further, we find a great amount of circumstantial evidence positively showing that the statements conform to the conditions of time and place, so far as we know them, this adds immensely to the weight of the testimony. We never can fill in all the background of any historical fact. But if the statement of it fits into the background as far as we can fill it in, we should accept the fact until positive contrary evidence is produced. No supposition can be more extravagant than that which Professor Barton seems to accept (which is that of the German critic, Meyer) that a Jew, more than a 1,000 years after the event, obtained in Babylon the amount of exact information concerning the conditions in Babylonia in Abraham's time, found in the fourteenth chapter of Genesis, and interpolated the story of Chedorlaomer's expedition into the background thus furnished. To entertain such a supposition discredits the prevalent critical scholarship, rather than the Sacred Scripture.

But present space forbids further enumeration of particulars. It is sufficient to say that while many more positive confirmations of the seemingly improbable statements of the sacred historians can be adduced, there have been no discoveries which necessarily contravene their statements. The cases already here enumerated relate to such widely separated times and places, and furnish explanations so unexpected, yet natural, to difficulties that have been thought insuperable, that their testimony cannot be ignored or rejected. That this history should be confirmed in so many cases and in such a remarkable manner by monuments uncovered 3,000 years after their erection, can be nothing else than providential. Surely, God has seen to it that the failing faith of these later days should not be left to grope in darkness. When the faith of so many was waning and many heralds of truth were tempted to speak with uncertain sound, the very stones have cried out with a voice that only the deaf could fail to hear. Both in the writing and in the preservation of the Bible we behold the handiwork of God.

CHRISTIANS AND THE BIBLE.

In reading a discourse given by Pastor Russell, of Peoples' Pulpit, New York, recently, I was pleased to see some of the teachings of the Prophet Joseph Smith given as facts by Mr. Russell. Certainly he does not mention the Prophet's name, and did not know he was agreeing with the Latter-day Saints. But, nevertheless, it is refreshing to hear a man like Mr. Russell admit facts that many ministers of the gospel are cognizant of but have not the courage to advance.

After saying many had turned away from God and the Bible, and still were numbered as Christians, he continues thus: "The difficulty with the present situation is that we have stupidly and blunderingly misread the Bible. We have twisted what we did read, and picked out certain portions which pleased best our own fancies and supported best our various creeds. * * * The confusion of Christendom is our reward."

Is not that just what the elders of this Church have been preaching for years? It is exactly.

Joseph Smith was told by Christ (when Joseph received his first vision) that the ministers of the gospel were "teaching for doctrine the commandments of men." Listen to what Mr. Russell says: "The fault of Christendom has been the rejection of the Divine plan and the acceptance of a human plan." Exactly so. This is no new teaching to the Latter-day Saints. They know it, because they have received the light; but does the Christian world, as a whole, admit the fact? No, only a few men like Mr. Russell do that.

Mr. Russell said the people needed to be converted. Converted to what? Why, to the gospel of Christ. Many say they are converted, but it is to the human plan, not to the Divine.

Christians have turned away from the main teaching of the Bible, and have "twisted" the scriptures to suit their own ends.

The question might be asked: How are we different from the rest of Christendom? Peter says, "that no prophecy of the scriptures is of any private interpretation," because "holy men of God spake as they were moved by the Holy Ghost." If the scriptures are of no private interpretation, how are they to be interpreted? Why, as they were written, by the Spirit of God. Paul tells us no man can know the things of God except it be by the Spirit of God. All right then, how are we to get that Spirit? How did the saints of old receive it? To the law and to the testimony. In Acts, eighth chapter, we are told how this Spirit, or Holy Ghost, was conferred. It was given by the laying on of hands. When? After the people had repented of their sins, and had been baptised by immersion for the remission of those sins. Now, then, what is the difference between us and the balance of Christendom? Just this, that we have obeyed these principles of the gospel, and have received the Holy Ghost by the laying on of hands. Also, we have had light given to us by God through His chosen prophets here upon the earth. Through these men, inspired of God, we receive instruction from time to time.

Can Christendom claim to be in this condition? I think not.

To any who are not of us, but who read these lines I would say—do not turn away from the Bible, or "twist" its teachings to suit your purpose, but as Christ says, "Search the scriptures, for in them ye think ye have eternal life." Do not do, as the Jews did, reject the very thing the scriptures bear record of.

39 The Woodlands, HAROLD W. LANGTON.
Birkenhead.

JUDGE NOT.

Judge not.
What looks to thy dim eyes a stain,
In God's pure light may only be
A scar, brought from some well-won field,
Where thou would'st only faint and yield.

THE LATTER-DAY SAINTS' MILLENNIAL STAR.

THURSDAY, DECEMBER 15, 1910.

JOSEPH SMITH, THE PROPHET.

"It is by no means improbable that some future textbook for the use of generations yet unborn, will contain a question something like this: What historical American of the nineteenth century has exerted the most powerful influence upon the destinies of his countrymen? And it is by no means impossible that the answer to that interrogatory may be thus written: *Joseph Smith, the Mormon Prophet.* And the reply, absurd as it doubtless seems to most men now living, may be an obvious commonplace to their descendants. History deals in paradoxes quite as startling as this. The man who established a religion in this age of free debate, who was and is to-day accepted by hundreds of thousands as a direct emissary from the Most High—such a rare human being is not to be disposed of by pelting his memory with unsavory epithets."—From Josiah Quincy's Book, *Figures of the Past.*

By the time we issue from the press again we shall be on the eve of the 23rd of December, the one hundred and fifth anniversary of the advent into the world of Joseph Smith, the Prophet, universally admitted to be a most remarkable man—hence the pertinency at this time of special reference to his memory.

Josiah Quincy was a traveler and author of note, and although his book, *Figures of the Past*, was not published until 1882, the materials used were gathered in the form of copious notes, or data, in the spring of 1844 while Mr. Quincy was visiting the prophet at Nauvoo, only forty-three days before the martyrdom. The quotation with which this article opens is only an extract from a chapter or two devoted to the great leader and the thriving city which he founded, but it forms a sort of conclusion of the matter as seen through the eyes of one not blinded by prejudice; one who had traveled and who knew men.

A characteristic of Joseph Smith which never failed to impress impressible people of all creeds, or of no creed, was the splendid spirit of self-reliance exhibited under peculiarly discouraging and provoking circumstances. Journalists of his time were wont to say, for lack of a better comparison, that he possessed the "moral courage of a Mahommet." He possessed that moral courage without the fanaticism so usual in religious revivalists. And he was a religious revivalist in a way, too, but his way was calm and decorous, for he lived in an atmosphere of assurance the like of which no man had felt since the apostles of the primitive Church sealed their testimonies with their blood.

At the time Mr. Quincy's estimate was written, the success of the work established by the Prophet was problematical in the eyes of the world. He had made great claims: for instance, that his name should be had for good and for evil in all the world, and that the Church which he had established would flourish and become mighty, but in 1844 there was little enough outward evidence of the fulfilment of these great predictions. Nauvoo, founded about five years previously, under distressing circumstances, the people in poverty and sickness, was just beginning to assume an appearance of thrift and stability. Enemies of the leader were in constant conspiracy to effect his death, thinking thereby to deal a telling blow to the community which by its strict morality and fervent religious spirit, put them (these enemies) to shame. A sovereign State (Missouri) had refused to grant the saints assistance to repel mob violence, or even to permit self-defense—an attitude on the part of the commonwealth which exhibited a grossness of injustice scarcely equalled in the history of civilization. It was, indeed, a remarkable personality that could face the world under these circumstances and boldly declare the ultimate triumph of the work he represented. And when it is understood that at the very time of Quincy's visit, the Prophet had strong presentiments of his impending martyrdom, his calm assurance could not fail to impress all who were brought within the pale of his activities. Men who did not recognize his true mission stood nonplussed in contemplation of his character, for he presented a problem in mental and spiritual phenomena which defied all attempts at solution by the application of any psychological formula known to men of the day. There was no place in their elaborate systems for the classification of those divine attributes which made him a prophet, seer, and revelator. Worldly-wise men had proclaimed long and loud the utter cessation of revelation, so what need had students of human nature to attempt analysis of that influence upon the mind? Thus a prophet was a puzzle.

Elder John Henry Evans, in the opening paragraphs of chapter six of his book, *One Hundred Years of Mormonism*, uses an illustration which will be appreciated by the reader in connection with the preceding observations in this article. We quote:

"In the *Arabian Nights' Entertainment*, there is a story of a man who approached the door of a cave, 'a large chamber, well lighted from the top, and in it all sorts of provisions, rich bales of silk stuff, brocade and carpeting, gold and silver ingots in great heaps, and money in bags.' Now, Cassim—for that was the man's name—had greed and murder in his heart, which, together with the excitement he was under at finding such a rich treasure, made him forget the charm by which alone it might be obtained. 'Open barley,' he cried, 'open rye,' and so on till he exhausted his memory of the grains. 'Sesame' was the only one he could not remember, and 'Sesame' was the only word to which the door of this chamber of fabulous wealth flew open. And so it was to him as if it had not been.'

"It is something after this fashion that a great many people approach the door of the treasures of truth locked up in the soul of 'Mormonism's' earthly founder. The hate and bitterness and evil purposes lurking in their hearts, or a predisposition to make the facts fit their theory, often indeed showing upon their faces and general appearance, cause them to forget the charmed words by which alone that treasure-house will pour forth its precious contents. 'Open impostor,' they cry out in their overflowing venom, 'Open deceiver, false prophet, base man!' But to them the door remains forever sealed. It opens only to the 'Man of God!'"

It's easy enough to understand the lack of appreciation of Joseph Smith, on the part of professors of religion. To acknowledge him would require that they confess their errors, swallow their pride, *and give up their "livings."* Some few have done this, but it would be a great deal to expect of them as a class. They did the logical thing according to their code—opposed the admission of revelation into religion.

"But why," some one may ask, "did not men like Josiah Quincy—and many such formed the prophet's acquaintance—readily perceive in him the Man of God? You say that he was distinctly outspoken, telling in plain language, even as did the Son of God, who he was and just how he might be understood. You point to these individuals yourselves as men of open minds and keen perceptive faculties as witness the unprejudiced testimonials they have left on record. Why were they puzzled?"

It isn't given to man to search the innermost recesses of his brother's heart and mind, but St. Paul, in writing to the Corinthian saints, gives us a striking example of cause and effect. "For what man knoweth the things of a man, save the spirit of man which is in him? even so the things of God knoweth no man, but the Spirit of God. * * * the natural man receiveth not the things of the Spirit of God: for they are foolishness unto him: neither can he know them, because they are spiritually discerned." (I. Cor. 2:11, 14.) Shall we say, then, that to the low ebb of their spirituality we ascribe their perceptive limitations? That would be a charitable disposition of the question—and it is scriptural.

None of the evidences by which a prophet is judged were lacking in him. He stands up admirably under the test prescribed by Moses. "When a prophet speaketh in the name of the Lord, if the thing follow not nor come to pass, that is the thing which the Lord hath not spoken, but the prophet hath spoken it presumptuously." (Deut. 18: 22.) That phase of the prophetic function which pertains to teaching and explaining the will of God as already revealed, found him quite equal to the occasion. His elucidation of the Scriptures and his delineation of the pre-existent state, transcend in clearness and comprehensiveness, the work of any previous prophet, save only the Redeemer. And, the record of his life and death bears the holy seal of martyrdom. "For where a testament is, there must also of necessity be the death of the testator. For a testament is of force after men are dead: otherwise it is of no strength at all while the testator liveth. Whereupon neither the first testament was dedicated without blood." (Heb. 9: 16-18.) Many have testified of his manly qualities, being in possession of the spirit of man, but lacking the spirit by which Godly attributes are measured and understood, they gave him up as a puzzle. To quote once more from Elder Evans:

"To reconcile the apparent contradictions in his life will never be possible by assuming him to be a false prophet, a deceiver, a hypocrite, a fraud, and so on. This only increases the difficulty for honest men wishing to arrive at the truth. The only solution of the problem is to presuppose that Joseph was a true prophet sent of God. Then everything of a puzzling or enigmatical character that enemies imagine they detected in him, will at once disappear."

"The Seer! The Seer! Joseph the Seer!
O, how I love his memory dear!
The just and wise, the pure and free,
A father he was and is to me.
Let friends now rage in their dark hour—
No matter, he is beyond their power."

S. N. L.

THE ecstacy of faith, hope, uplift and sublime strength is highly contagious, and sick people—those with nervous disorders—coming under its influence are often made to stand erect, unsupported, leap with joy, and are well. Thoughtful physicians know and admit the wonderful effects of mind on mind, and of mind over matter. Most physical ills proceed from disordered imagination, and in passing, it may be well to state this fact. Imagination is the most intensely real and actual thing of which we know. The pains and sorrows of the imagination are the only real ones and all the joys and delights of men are matters of spirit. All appetites, with their attractions and revulsions are matters of the imagination. The extent to which one highly imaginative individual of sterling purity of purpose and sublime power may benefit the weary, the depressed, the sorely stricken and the sick, we do not know. But these cures and benefits are not miraculous, they are all under some distinct, invariable Law which as yet we imperfectly understand. It is part of the great unknown.—HUBBARD.

NORTHAMPTON CHAPEL DEDICATED.

THE newly acquired chapel at Northampton was dedicated Sunday, the 11th inst., with appropriate ceremonies. Besides the traveling elders, J. E. Wiggill and Albert Smith, President Rudger Clawson and Elder S. Norman Lee were present from Liverpool, also President Thomas F. Greenwood of the Birmingham conference and Conference Clerk John M. Young were there from Birmingham. The house has been entirely renovated since it was purchased last summer, and now presents a very neat and comfortable appearance, a delightful place of meeting for the saints of Northampton.

Sunday School was held in the morning at 10:30. Instead of the regular class work being taken up, the meeting was devoted to singing and speaking. Elder S. Norman Lee recounted some of his impressions of Sunday School in boyhood days. President Clawson told of some of his experiences in the Church in connection with Sunday Schools, remarking upon their great importance as a place of education for the children especially.

The services in the afternoon, which were public, commenced at three o'clock. Elder John M. Young spoke of the power of love in uplifting humanity. President Clawson developed for the benefit of the saints, the doctrine of salvation for the dead. Elder S. Norman Lee and Sister May Freeman sang as a duet, "Jesus Lover of My Soul."

The evening meeting commenced promptly at 6 o'clock. Elder S. Norman Lee was the first speaker. He pointed out that it was a difficult matter to say of any one principle of the gospel, This is the most important of all. All were important and could not be dispensed with. President Greenwood spoke of the manner in which the house was secured, and congratulated the people upon its possession. Elder S. Norman Lee and Sister May Freeman sang, "This House We Dedicate." President Clawson then offered the dedicatory prayer, during which there was the utmost quiet in the room. The meeting was well attended by saints and many investigators, who listened very attentively. After the prayer, the congregation sang, "Redeemer of Israel." President Clawson spoke upon the necessity of good works with faith, drawing many plain passages in support from the Holy Scriptures. The services during all of the day were very pleasant indeed, and the elders and saints of Northampton consider themselves fortunate in the matter of a meeting place.

A LIFE that only marks time, that does not march forward, cannot be a victorious life. The more battles won, the more victorious the forward movement. If a man gains but an inch a day against temptation and privation he is a growing, conquering disciple. The man who stands still is a useless, half-defeated one.

FROM THE MISSION FIELD.

Successful Choir Concert.—On Saturday night, December 3rd, 1910, the choir in Nottingham (Nottingham conference) gave a very successful concert in the Mechanics' Hall. Several of the artists were professionals. The hall was almost filled, there being about seventy-five strangers present. Every one seemed pleased with the results, and several strangers were heard to say they were surprised to hear such good talent among the "Mormons."

Baptisms.—A baptismal service was held at Burnley Central Baths (Liverpool conference) November 26th, 1910, at which four persons were baptised by Elder Thomas Walton.

Eight applicants for baptism had the ordinance performed Sunday, December 4th, 1910, at High Street Baths, Birmingham (Birmingham conference). Those officiating were Elders H. C. Swainston and A. R. Howard.

At a baptismal service held December 4th, 1910, at "Deseret," South Tottenham (London conference), Elders J. H. Eccles, Jr., and J. W. Saville baptised two converts.

District Meeting.—Upwards of a hundred people attended a district meeting held in the Cross Hall, Halesowen (Birmingham conference), Sunday, December 4th, 1910, of which nearly half were investigators and strangers. The speakers were President T. F. Greenwood, Elders John M. Young and Elisha Peck, Jr. The choir did some very creditable work, and the good spirit which prevailed at the meeting caused much comment among the visitors. On Monday evening, at the same place, a social and tea was held in honor of Elder Elisha Peck, Jr., Sisters Jennie Patrick and Florence Carter and Brother Joseph Parsons, all of whom are sailing for America on December 8th. Practically the same audience assembled on Monday night, and a good time was reported by all concerned.

Releases and Departures.—The following named missionaries have been honorably released and sailed for home December 8th, 1910, per s.s. *Dominion*: From Great Britain—W. H. Callahan, Albert J. Hunt, James B. George, E. W. Williams, John H. Eccles, Jr., E. M. Wright, Elijah Gilbert, Paul Condie, Henry E. King, James Palmer, Elisha Peck, Jr., William S. Isgreen. From Scandinavia—Hans P. Anderson, William D. Norman, Charles H. Sorensen, L. M. Brienholt. From Sweden—Gus E. Oscarson, Albert Capson. From Switzerland and Germany—John Grunder, John P. Künzler. From the Netherlands—Ira Q. Rice, Fred. R. O. Acord. With the company were forty-three emigrants in charge of Elders Henry E. King, Elisha Peck, Jr., and William D. Norman. The following named missionaries were honorably released and sailed for home

December 10th, 1910, per s.s. *Baltic*: From Great Britain—Cyrus W. Card, David M. Powelson. From the Netherlands—Romelyn Adams, Claude A. Woolley, John J. Millard. From Switzerland and Germany—George H. Gowans, John P. Benson, William L. Hansen.

Arrivals.—The following named missionaries for the European mission arrived December 10th, 1910, per s.s. *Laurentic*: Walter Henry Allington, Holliday, Utah; John J. Whetton, Lawrence Poulton, J. Thurman Smith, John Berntson, Carl O. Youngberg, Lawrence C. Monson, Peter O. Peterson, Gustave E. Sjoberg, Salt Lake City; Sarah A. Howard, Woods Cross, Utah; Leslie A. Merrill, Preston, Idaho; Moroni W. Green, Wellsville, Utah; Parley J. Welch, William J. Roberts, Paradise, Utah; Olof Anderson, Ogden, Utah; Frederick Mickelson, Shelley, Idaho; James Anderson, Bingham, Idaho; Arthur L. Olsen, Carl J. Olsson, Logan, Utah; John P. Erickson, John W. Anderson, Otto Johnson, Grantsville, Utah; Joseph F. Hintze, Big Cottonwood, Utah; Gottlieb Blatter, Ammon, Idaho.

Appointments.—The missionaries who arrived for the British mission, December 10th, 1910, have been appointed to labor in the following conferences: Leslie A. Merrill, J. Thurman Smith, Bristol; Sarah A. Howard, Birmingham; Parley J. Welch, William J. Roberts, Irish; W. H. Allington, Liverpool; Lawrence Poulton, John J. Whetton, Moroni W. Green, London.

Successful Socials.—A very enjoyable social was held at 14 Picardy Place, Edinburgh (Scottish conference), November 30th, 1910, in honor of Elder William Sidney Isgreen, who has been honorably released to return home. A nice program was rendered, many friends taking part. A dainty lunch was served and games played. Elder Isgreen was presented with a beautiful Scotch traveling rug by the elders, saints and friends of Edinburgh, in which branch he has labored for the past seventeen months.

On Wednesday, November 30th, 1910, a successful social was held at 144 George Street West, Hyde (Manchester conference), in honor of Elder J. E. Layne, who has been honorably released to return to Zion. A large number of saints and friends were present. An interesting program was rendered, after which refreshments were served, and all had an enjoyable time. The branch presented Elder Layne with a traveling rug and a dinner cruet. The choir, which Elder Layne has been leading for the past eight months, presented him with a gentleman's dressing case.

A musical and literary entertainment was given at Sparkbrook Chapel, Birmingham branch (Birmingham conference), Saturday, December 3rd, 1910, for the benefit of the Sunday Schools. It was a success artistically and financially. The funds raised will be devoted to the interests of the children. The superintendency of the schools will arrange for a repetition of the delightful entertainment at the Wretham Road Assembly Room in the near future.

SUNDAY SCHOOL LESSON FOR THEOLOGICAL DEPARTMENT.

LESSON IV.—THE ATONEMENT.

Text: We believe that through the atonement of Christ, all mankind may be saved, by obedience to the laws and ordinances of the Gospel.—*Articles of Faith, III.*

I. NATURE OF THE ATONEMENT.

1. Meaning of the term—*at-one-ment*, "denoting reconciliation, or the bringing into agreement of those who have been estranged." (See Romans 5: 10, 11; note the marginal reading "reconciliation" for "atonement" in reference Bible.
2. A necessary sequence of Adam's transgression (I. Cor. 15: 21, 22; see also "Mediation and Atonement," pp. 148, 149.
3. A vicarious sacrifice. (a) Observe that vicarious offerings were required under the Mosaic law, e. g., the altar victim and the scape-goat. (Leviticus 4, and 16: 20-22.) (b) Such offerings were required of Adam (P. of G. P., Moses 5: 5, 6.) Such were a prototype of the later atoning death of Christ (last reference, verses 7 and 8.) (d) Vicarious nature of the atonement declared. (Doc. and Cov. 19: 16-19. See further John 3: 14-17; Luke 9: 56; I. John 2: 1, 2; I. Timothy 2: 5, 6; B. of M., I. Nephi 10: 5, 6; 11: 32, 33; II. Nephi 2: 6-8; Mosiah 4: 6-9; Alma 34: 11-16.)

II. CHRIST'S SACRIFICE WAS VOLUNTARY.

1. His offer made and accepted at the Council in Heaven. (See Lesson 3, "The Fall," IV.)
2. His power over death—no man could take His life without His surrender. (John 10: 17, 18; see also 5: 26, 27; compare Matt. 26: 53, 54.)
3. Inspired by love. (a) For His Father, whose will He sought to do. (b) For mankind, whose redemption He sought to accomplish. (See Luke 23: 34; John 3: 16, 17; I. John 4: 9.)

III. THE ATONEMENT FOREORDAINED AND FORETOLD.

1. (I. Peter 1: 19, 20; see "Mediation and Atonement," p. 97; P. of G. P., Moses 6: 51-60.) Note the Savior's personal application of prophecies concerning His atoning sacrifice. (Luke 24: 27, 45, 46; see especially B. of M., Ether 3: 14, 8-16; compare I. Nephi 10: 3-11.

IV. Extent of the Atonement.

1. General effect—universal redemption from the effects of the Fall; universal resurrection of the dead. (In addition to Scriptures already cited, see Rom. 5: 18; I. Tim. 2: 5, 6; B. of M., Mosiah 4: 7; Doc. and Cov. 76: 42; also John 11: 25; 5: 28, 29: compare Doc. and Cov. 76: 17; I. Cor. 15: 22; Rev. 20: 12, 13.)
2. Special effect—individual salvation provided on specific conditions. (Heb. 5: 9; see especially B. of M., Mosiah 3: 11, 12.)

General reference: "The Articles of Faith, Lecture IV., pp. 76-97.

BEAUTY.

There is beauty everywhere
To the "seeing" eye;
Rainbow hues in every tear,
Music in a sigh.

There is beauty in the wind
When it's blowing wild;
There is beauty in the mind
Of a little child.

Beauty lives in everything
On the earth below;
That beauty reigns above as king
Let ev'ry mortal know.

Gateshead-on-Tyne. Aubrey Parker.

DIED.

Saxton.—At Eastwood, November 14th, 1910, Emmanuel Saxton, born January 9th, 1826, baptised and confirmed January 28th, 1849. Deceased was President of Eastwood branch (Nottingham conference) for about forty years.

Pattison.—At Middlesbro,' Yorkshire, England, November 17th, 1910, Stephen Pattison. Deceased was born at South Shields, Durham County, May 1st, 1867.

Holden.—At Nelson, Lancashire, November 23rd, 1910, Mrs. Emma Holden, aged 66 years. Deceased was baptised November 27th, 1909, by Elder Mark H. Greene, and was a faithful Latter-day Saint.

CONTENTS:

EDITED, PRINTED AND PUBLISHED BY RUDGER CLAWSON, 295 EDGE LANE,
LIVERPOOL:
FOR SALE IN ALL THE CONFERENCES OF THE CHURCH OF JESUS CHRIST OF LATTER-DAY SAINTS IN GREAT BRITAIN.

CPSIA information can be obtained
at www.ICGtesting.com
Printed in the USA
BVHW04*1051051018
529387BV00010B/53/P

9 780265 586440